STARK LIBRARY NOV - - 2022

CHANCE THE RAPPER

RAPPING ★ SUPERSTAR

REBECCA FELIX

Big Buddy Books

An Imprint of Abdo Publishing
abdobooks.com

ABDOBOOKS.COM

Published by Abdo Publishing, a division of ABDO, PO Box 398166, Minneapolis, Minnesota 55439. Copyright © 2022 by Abdo Consulting Group, Inc. International copyrights reserved in all countries. No part of this book may be reproduced in any form without written permission from the publisher. Big Buddy Books™ is a trademark and logo of Abdo Publishing.

Printed in the United States of America, North Mankato, Minnesota

052021
092021

Design: Kelly Doudna, Mighty Media, Inc.
Production: Mighty Media, Inc.
Editor: Liz Salzmann
Cover Photograph: Jordan Strauss/AP Images
Interior Photographs: Ashlee Rezin/Sun-Times/AP Images, pp. 21, 29 (bottom); Charles Rex Arbogast/AP Images, pp. 27, 29 (center); Jason Mendez/AP Images, pp. 1, 28; Jeff Kravitz/Getty Images, p. 7; NASA/Bill Ingalls/Flickr, p. 13; Shutterstock Images, pp. 5, 9, 11, 15, 17, 23, 29 (top); WENN Rights Ltd./Alamy, p. 19; Xavier Collin/Image Press Agency/AP Images, p. 25

Library of Congress Control Number: 2020949942

Publisher's Cataloging-in-Publication Data

Names: Felix, Rebecca, author.
Title: Chance the Rapper: rapping superstar / by Rebecca Felix
Other title: rapping superstar
Description: Minneapolis, Minnesota : Abdo Publishing, 2022 | Series: Superstars | Includes online resources and index.
Identifiers: ISBN 9781532195655 (lib. bdg.) | ISBN 9781098216382 (ebook)
Subjects: LCSH: Chance the Rapper (Chancelor Bennett)--Juvenile literature. | Rap musicians--United States--Biography--Juvenile literature. | Singers--United States--Biography--Juvenile literature. | Rap (Music)--Juvenile literature. | African American musicians--Juvenile literature.
Classification: DDC 782.42164--dc23

CONTENTS

Chance the Rapper · 4
Chicago Childhood · 6
10 Day · 10
Acid Rap & Open Mike · 14
Surf & Charity · 18
Album & Awards · 20
Screen Projects · 24
Chance the Do-Gooder · 26
Timeline · 28
Glossary · 30
Online Resources · 31
Index · 32

CHANCE THE RAPPER

Chance the Rapper is not just a rap superstar. He is also a singer, songwriter, and actor. Chance is known for being an independent artist. He is also passionate about helping others.

> 'Chance the Rapper' is many things. I'm constantly evolving.

Chance chose the stage name Chance the Rapper to show that being a rapper was something to be proud of.

CHICAGO CHILDHOOD

Chancelor Johnathan Bennett was born on April 16, 1993, in Chicago, Illinois. His parents are Ken Williams-Bennett and Lisa Bennett. Ken worked as an **aide** to several politicians. One of these was Harold Washington, Chicago's first Black mayor. Chance has a younger brother, Taylor. Taylor is also a rapper.

In 2017, Chance (*right*) attended a Grammy Awards party with his parents.

Music was a big **influence** on young Chance. He listened to pop stars such as Michael Jackson. Chance also liked gospel, jazz, and R&B music.

Chance discovered rap when he heard Kanye West on the radio. Chance was just nine years old. Soon he was writing his own raps. By age 13, Chance knew he was going to be a rapper.

> Kanye took me from a kid who listened to music to a kid who lived music.

Kanye West also grew up in Chicago. Chance would one day work with West.

 10 DAY

In high school, Chance often rapped at **open mic** nights. A man named Brother Mike held these events for Chicago youth.

In 2011, Chance got in trouble at school. He was suspended for 10 days. Chance used this time to record songs.

In April 2012, Chance released a **mixtape** called *10 Day*. He posted it on the streaming site DatPiff. People could download the mixtape for free.

Chance recorded *10 Day* at YOUmedia in Chicago's Harold Washington Library.

The **mixtape** was a success. DatPiff users downloaded it more than 400,000 times! And many online music writers posted positive reviews of it.

Rapper Childish Gambino also took notice of *10 Day*. He asked Chance to perform on his song "They Don't Like Me." Childish Gambino also asked Chance to be the opening act on his 2012 Camp Gambino tour!

Childish Gambino's real name is Donald Glover. Besides being a rapper, he is also an actor, comedian, and writer.

ACID RAP & OPEN MIKE

After the Camp Gambino tour, Chance recorded more songs. In April 2013, he posted the **mixtape** *Acid Rap* on DatPiff. *Acid Rap* was a hit. It was downloaded more than 1 million times!

That year Chance also began dating Kirsten Corley. He had first seen her at a party when he was nine years old.

Singer and songwriter BJ the Chicago Kid was one of several artists who worked on *Acid Rap* with Chance.

In 2014, Brother Mike died. Chance and a friend decided to take over his **open mic** program. They called it Open Mike in Brother Mike's honor. Chance brought famous rappers such as Kanye West to Open Mike.

Also in 2014, Chance was in an **episode** of the **animated** TV show *Black Dynamite*. Chance voiced the character of reggae singer Bob Marley.

Actor Kym Whitley voiced Honeybee, one of the main characters in *Black Dynamite*.

SURF & CHARITY

In 2015, Chance joined Donnie Trumpet & The Social Experiment. The group released the album *Surf*. And in September, Chance became a father. He and Corley welcomed daughter Kensli.

SUPERSTAR ★ SCOOP
In 2016, Chance helped found SocialWorks. This charity helps Chicago youth gain skills for success. SocialWorks provides art, music, and other programs.

Donnie Trumpet (*left*) and Chance the Rapper performed at Taste of Chicago in 2016.

ALBUM & AWARDS

On May 13, 2016, Chance released *Coloring Book*. By this time, many **labels** wanted to sign him. But Chance refused. But, he did make a deal with **technology** company Apple.

Apple offered Chance $500,000 to stream *Coloring Book* first on Apple Music. After two weeks, he could also stream it on other sites.

Chance almost always wears a baseball cap. Since 2016, his caps have had the number 3 on them because *Coloring Book* was his third mixtape.

Coloring Book made history. It started at Number 8 on the *Billboard* 200 List. It was the first streaming-only album to make the list.

In 2017, *Coloring Book* won Best Rap Album at the Grammy Awards. It was the first streaming-only album to win a Grammy!

Chance also became the first **solo** male rapper to win Best New Artist. Chance's third Grammy was Best Rap Performance for the song "No Problem."

Besides three Grammy Awards, Chance also won three BET Awards in 2017. He attended the BET Awards with his mother.

SCREEN PROJECTS

Over the next two years, Chance appeared in movies and on TV. He was in the 2018 horror movie *Slice*.

In 2019, Chance cohosted several **episodes** of the rap talent show *Rhythm + Flow*. He also had a small part in the Disney movie *The Lion King*. In August, Chance and Corley welcomed a second daughter, Marli.

Corley (*left*) and Chance brought Kensli to *The Lion King* movie opening in Los Angeles, California.

CHANCE THE DO-GOODER

In addition to his music, Chance also **focuses** on **activism** and helping others. In April 2020, he earned the UNICEF Chicago Humanitarian Award. It honors people who work to help children.

What's next for this rapper who is so much more? Chance says he just wants to be remembered as a good person.

In 2017, Chance performed at an event to support the Obama Foundation. The organization was founded by former president Barack Obama (*left*) and Michelle Obama (*center*).

TIMELINE

1993 — Chancelor Johnathan Bennett was born on April 16, 1993, in Chicago, Illinois.

2011 — Chance was suspended from school. He used the time to create the mixtape *10 Day*.

2012 — Chance toured with Childish Gambino.

2013 — Chance began dating Kirsten Corley and released a second mixtape, *Acid Rap*.

Chance released *Surf* with Donnie Trumpet & The Social Experiment. He and Corley welcomed daughter Kensli.

Chance won three Grammy Awards.

Chance earned the UNICEF Chicago Humanitarian Award for his activism.

2015 **2017** **2020**

2016 **2019**

Chance helped found the charity organization SocialWorks. He released the album *Coloring Book*.

Chance and Corley welcomed a second daughter, Marli.

29

GLOSSARY

activism—working for or speaking up about a cause or issue you believe in.

aide—a person who acts as an assistant.

animated—made using drawings instead of live actors.

episode—one show in a series of shows.

focus (FOH-kuhs)—to give attention to.

influence—to have an effect on something.

label—a company that produces musical recordings.

mixtape—a collection of songs or other recordings that is usually given away for free.

open mic—an event where anyone can perform.

solo—a performance by a single person.

technology (tehk-NAH-luh-jee)—related to the use of science for practical purposes.

ONLINE RESOURCES

To learn more about Chance the Rapper, please visit **abdobooklinks.com** or scan this QR code. These links are routinely monitored and updated to provide the most current information available.

INDEX

Acid Rap, 14, 15, 28
acting, 4, 16, 24
activism, 4, 18, 26, 27
Apple Music, 20
awards, 7, 22, 23, 26, 29

birth, 6, 28
BJ the Chicago Kid, 15
Black Dynamite, 16, 17
Brother Mike, 10, 16

California, 25
Chicago, 6, 9, 10, 11, 15, 18, 19, 26, 28, 29
childhood, 6, 8, 10, 11
Childish Gambino, 12, 13, 14, 28
Coloring Book, 20, 21, 22, 29

DatPiff, 10, 12, 14
Disney, 24
Donnie Trumpet & The Social Experiment, 18, 29

education, 10, 28

family, 6, 7, 14, 18, 23, 24, 25, 28, 29
Jackson, Michael, 8

Lion King, The, 24, 25

Marley, Bob, 16
mixtapes, 10, 11, 12, 14, 20, 21, 22, 28, 29

Obama, Barack, 27
Obama, Michelle, 27
Obama Foundation, 27
Open Mike, 16

Rhythm + Flow, 24

Slice, 24
SocialWorks, 18, 29
Surf, 18, 29

10 Day, 10, 11, 12, 28
Trumpet, Donnie, 18, 19, 29

Washington, Harold, 6, 11
West, Kanye, 8, 9, 16

3 1333 05173 9561